Disclaimer

Freshwater & Totland Archive Group formed in 2010, a voluntary group aiming to record, preserve and share the local history of our villages and to keep alive the memories of those who made them what they are.

This is not intended as a precise history book; the contents have been researched from generously donated material and from many varied sources, some of which are anecdotal. The Group has sought to identify and acknowledge copyright ownership but this has not always proved possible. Copyright owners are invited to contact the Group so that acknowledgements can be made in any future edition.

With such a rich local history we have merely scratched the surface in this publication but we hope it may encourage others to delve into the local records. If you have information to share or would like to make comments or to learn more about the Group, please contact Freshwater & Totland Archive Group, c/o Freshwater Library.

Visit: www.archiverescue.com

Email: archiverescue@hotmail.co.uk

Front-cover photograph: Detail of postcard of School Green, circa 1904

First published in 2014 by Beachy Community Books

This book was created by Freshwater & Totland Archive Group (Archive Rescue) on a Beachy Books Community Book Publishing Project created and delivered by Philip Bell. For more information visit: www.beachybooks.com

FRESHWATER REFLECTIONS

School Green, Freshwater

School Green circa 1910, with Moa Place (left) and Hokitika, Elliott's, the
Assembly Rooms and Royal Standard (right)

Archive Rescue

THE S...

FORT VICTORIA
WESTHILL LANE

NORTON

FORT ALBERT

HALLETT'S SHO...

MONKS LANE

HILL LANE
NORTON GREEN
PIXLEY HILL
COLWELL ROAD

COPSE LANE

COLWELL BAY
Long Beach

COLWELL CHINE Rd

COLWELL Rd

HEATHFIELD Rd

GOLDEN HILL FORT

FRESHWATER

All Saints School

K.. M F..

Baptist Ch.
Colwell Bay Inn

FORT WARDEN

COLWELL COMMON Rd

COLWELL LANE
SILCOMBE LANE
PRINCES Rd
Prince of Wales
HIGH St

FRESHWATER LIBRARY

HOOK.. H..

The Vine
The Royal Standard

SCHOOL GREEN ROAD

TOTLAND BAY

TOTLAND PIER

THE AVENUE
AVENUE Rd.

TENNYSON Rd.

MOA PLACE
Wesley
BROOKSIDE ROAD
TOILETS

CAR PARK

GRANVILLE Rd.

THE BROADWAY

TOTLAND

CLAYTON Rd.

QUEENS ROAD

West Wight Sports Centre
Health Centre

MADEIRA ROAD

COURT Rd.

CAMP ROAD

VICTORIA ROAD

EASTO..

The Waterfront

CLIFF Rd.

CHURCH HILL

WESTON Rd.
St.
St. SAVIOUR'S

HURST HILL

SUMMERS LANE

POUND GREEN

BLACKBR..

YORK Rd.

St. Saviours

BEDBURY LANE

GATE LANE

ALUM BAY NEW Rd.

WESTON LANE

Christchurch

WESTON

MIDDLETON
Farringford

St Agnes

DIMBOLA

FB Hote..

ALUM BAY OLD Rd.

The Highdown

MOONS HILL

F.. RED..

TO THE NEEDLES

TENNYSON'S MONUMENT

Contents

Freshwater and the Tuns

Recorded in the Domesday Book of 1086, the name Freshwater is thought to derive from a source of fresh water at Freshwater Bay where but for a narrow peninsula Freshwater would be an island in itself; indeed, separation from the remainder of the island was at one time considered with 'Freshwater Isle' becoming a refuge in the event of invasion. The spring at Freshwater Bay leads via Afton Marsh into the River Yar, which until as late as the 18th century was called the 'Freshwater'.

'About the year 1830, Freshwater must have been a large, very scattered agricultural district or village, boasting only one or two isolated buildings at the Bay, and one or two shops in School Green.' Hilda Emmerton

Originally stretching from the western side of the Yar to the Needles, Freshwater consisted of five 'tuns' or 'tons', an ancient name for farm. While Norton, Easton, Middleton and Weston remain, Sutton became known as Freshwater Gate, with 'Gate' referring to a 'gap' between Afton and Tennyson Downs or possibly a 'pass'. Totland, which includes Weston and part of old Middleton, became a separate Civil Parish in 1894, but the other three tuns are still within the Parish of Freshwater.

The Rectory (presently Seahorses), Victoria Road, pre 1900

The original Freshwater village developed around All Saints' Church, while the modern village grew from the old hamlet of School Green and was pretty much self-sufficient; most needs were catered for from cradle to grave, from birth in the home and later in nursing homes such as those in Princes

H. Dowty & Sons, the Forge and Royal Standard Hotel, circa 1900

Road, the Square and Pound Green, to building firms that also provided undertaking services.

Transport advanced from horse and carriage to bicycle and rail, then to coach, car and omnibus; doctors practised from surgeries in their homes and district nurses made rounds by bicycle or moped. Mail and newspapers were delivered on foot or bicycle, and groceries, bread, meat and milk were delivered to the door. Laundry was collected and returned by van, gardens were supplemented by allotments, local bobbies kept the peace and churches and chapels were well attended with rectors and chaplains living locally in rectory or manse.

Many worked on the land or in construction with farms and estates also providing housing, while well-to-do families in large houses employed staff 'in service' (those in the service of Mrs Julia Margaret Cameron were sometimes required to model for photographs). Retail businesses employed staff of all ages and a variety of services trained staff in office and management skills.

Practically any item a household might need could be found in a shop, with personal service and free delivery, and the village supported several blacksmiths, boot-menders and tailors.

Social events were provided by many and various organisations and included splendid annual regattas with beach competitions, sideshows,

Carnival Programme, 1954

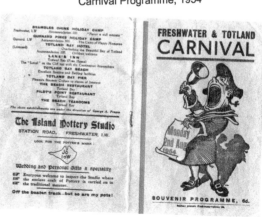

The Royal Standard Hotel after burning down in the early hours of 29th September 1905

dancing and fireworks, along with colourful carnivals that paraded to a travelling fairground, garden fêtes and sometimes a visit from the circus. Sport played a large part in village life with flourishing football, cricket, tennis, golf, boxing and bowling clubs, and many public houses provided indoor competitions and entertainment with darts, dominoes and cribbage.

The Gaiety and Palace Theatres were popular not only for meetings and early film shows, but also for local productions to raise funds for hospitals and local charities. Band concerts, choral events and recitals were complemented by local productions, which were enthusiastically received and well patronised. Assembly rooms combined with the Palace Theatre were used for meetings and functions until the building was destroyed by fire in 1929. In 1935 when the Regent Cinema and the Oak Tree café opened, queues would sometimes wind down to Moa Place; while the café closed in 1946 to be replaced by West

Regent Cinema Programme, 1958

The Regent Cinema and West Wight Pharmacy, circa 1960

Wight Pharmacy, the Regent Cinema continued to be a popular venue until 1962. West Wight's first supermarket, Richway, opened in 1969 on the Regent Cinema site.

With the development of holiday camps in the 1930s, West Wight holiday venues ranged from high-class hotels to camp sites in fields and family holidays became a valuable source of income to the area, bringing seasonal employment and of course trade to local businesses. It was a very sad day when the camps closed their doors and the campers departed.

Reginald Reader opened the by now derelict Gaiety as a lampshade factory in 1953. Besides being produced in the factory, lampshades were made by homeworkers, a very welcome source of extra housekeeping! As business grew, Readers moved to larger premises in The Avenue, where St Joseph's Private School had been built in 1902/3 by Belgian Arthur Buisseret. Requisitioned in 1940 while under the direction of Arthur's son Raphael, the school had been converted into a factory where Saunders Roe produced floats for Walrus seaplanes, also storing materials at the Gaiety. In 1956 the premises were again linked when Readers moved from old theatre to factory site.

Gaiety Theatre, built in 1916

More factories followed in the early 1960s with Millway Engineering at Golden Hill, Acorn Spring Works on the site of the Railway Station, and Matchmaker Wigs at Golden Hill in the late 1960s.

Salvation Army meeting at Vine Corner, 1920s

Churches

The Church has always figured very largely in Freshwater life, with past congregations of All Saints' Church making their way along Longhalves Lane or up a very different Hooke Hill from the one we see today. Written notes from a long-departed resident tell how the rutted surface was flattened only by the feet of parishioners and horses' hooves, and how at times a stone cracker would appear with a long handled hammer to split the larger portions while children laboriously trod in smaller stones only to see them washed out and carried off in the frequent rain.

All Saints' Church

Morning services were usually attended by the elite: trades people, the military, celebrated visitors such as those from Farringford, and by Mrs Cameron who would look around the church for suitable faces for her next 'study'. These elite would be the first to leave the church, presenting an opportunity for more humble parishioners to glimpse a new face and the fashions of the day, with those such as the Croziers, the Honourable Mrs Grosvenor Hood, Captain and Mrs Pixley, the Tennysons and Lady Hamond-Graeme holding impromptu social gatherings in front of the Church tower before boarding awaiting carriages.

Domestic staff from large houses attended church in the afternoon, often with children, and shivered in the stony shadows of the Church while when evening services were introduced they were lamp-lit. Many of these 'great and good' of Freshwater now lie in the Churchyard alongside those who once served and revered them.

With Sunday schools very popular, religious education and guidance were delivered by volunteer 'teachers' who were known, respected and mostly fondly thought of, with the annual Sunday School Outing eagerly anticipated, being an opportunity to travel by train or coach to parts of the Island never seen before or fleetingly remembered from previous outings.

'On Sundays the village was asleep save for the two Church bells... one called us to Church and announced the funerals, the other announced the parson's arrival at Church.'
Hilda Emmerton

Youth organisations flourished with Boys Brigade, Girls (Life) Brigade, Girl Guides, Sea Scouts, Scouts, Cubs and Brownies, all parading to various Churches on special occasions.

The old stone built Rectory in Victoria Road hosted splendid annual Church Fêtes where crowds of villagers enjoyed sports, games and entertainment, with tea and delicious homemade cake served in the Parish Hall. When this lovely old Rectory was sold in the 1950s a newer property in Afton Road became the clergy's home.

Apart from All Saints' Church, Freshwater supported various religious meeting houses, with an Iron Room in The Square preceding St Agnes' Church, a Good Templar's Hall in Victoria Road, the non-conformist Congregational Church in Guyer's Road, the Garrison Church of St Andrew's in Hill Lane, a Wesleyan Methodist Chapel at Brookside, Baptist Chapels at Middleton and Colwell, a Bible Christian Chapel at Norton Green, a Mission Hall in the High Street and a Brethren Meeting Place at Middleton and on Hooke Hill.

Wesleyan Chapel, with old thatched school house

Children were encouraged to donate toys at the annual toy service for children less fortunate than themselves, while missionary work and Children's Homes were supported by small offerings of coppers and perhaps the odd sixpenny piece. Records show the existence of a Coal Club where parishioners paid a small regular amount to receive fuel during winter months, and a Boot and Shoe Club to provide sturdy footwear for those in need.

Schools

Whilst education in Freshwater from the early 20th century is well recorded, perhaps less is known of schools set up in the homes of 'tutors' in earlier days. This writer of course having no personal memory of such establishments has learnt from anecdotes of 'schools' springing up and disappearing from the village at a surprising rate.

It is fairly well known that in 1714 local landowner David Urry of Afton Manor paid £20 per year for a teacher to give 16 children from poor families of Freshwater lessons in reading, writing and simple arithmetic. The school opened on 15th April 1715 with David Lacey appointed schoolmaster, while the last tutors were likely to have been George Lawrence and his wife Clarissa. A school is also thought to have stood on the site of the Vine Inn, where the Master was extremely deaf.

At Norlands House in Norton in the 1880s two non-conformist sisters, Mrs Mitchell and Mrs Carey, employed three teachers to teach the three Rs and needlework while they themselves taught Religious Knowledge. On the present site of Lansdowne the picturesque thatched Oak Cottage was the site of Ma'am Taylor's 'dame school' which burned down in about 1907/1909 and a small school at Stroud House run by two daughters of Mr Fortescue, a retired London baker, transferred over the road to a bedroom of Stroud Cottages for a short time while the girls' grandmother was ill.

A Miss Cooke, previously a teacher at Totland School and said to be a bad-tempered woman, taught music and opened a small school at The Elms in Victoria Road, then known as Temple's (now Applebarns), which later closed to re-open at Palmerston in The Square.

Maypole dancing at All Saints' School

Miss Hewett's school at Gladstone Cottage (now Easton Cottage) on the Mall also closed as it failed to prosper... only for Miss Hewett to return some years later with a sister said to have been a Governess in Russia, with impressive credentials and described as a very refined but extremely plain woman. The sisters opened a school at 1 Compton Villas, Guyers Road, while another school was opened for a short time in Shelley House by a retired national school teacher.

The National School opened in 1851, starting children on the path to becoming educated and sociable, with some going on to become pupil teachers in the school where they themselves had been educated. A small Council School built in Queens Road in 1906 was enlarged in 1938, with pupils attending St Saviour's and the National, now All Saints', School until completion in 1939; in 1955 a more modern kitchen and dining room were included in a new wing of this renamed West Wight County Secondary School, with smaller additions made before the closure of the again renamed West Wight Middle School in 2011, and its demolition in 2014.

The Railway Line

While goods trains ran on the Isle of Wight Central Railway's Freshwater–Newport line from 1888, Freshwater Station was opened to passengers by directors Messrs E. Granville Ward JP, E. Fox, G.H. Hogan and Lt.-Col. J. Walker on 20th July 1889, enabling a scenic journey in comparative comfort when making purchases and conducting business in the distant market town of Newport. Smaller stations at Yarmouth, Ningwood, Calbourne and Carisbrooke Halt were later supplemented by Sir John Simeon's private Watchingwell Halt when it became public in 1923 and all Island railways merged as Southern Railway.

'On cold winter mornings if I was early, my friend's engine driver father would invite me to "step up into the engine and warm your hands, mate".' Bob Acheson

Freshwater village saw Doves Lane renamed Station Road, with business properties developing in the vicinity of the Railway Station. The single platform was lengthened four times to accommodate longer trains and it was planned that the line should be continued to Totland Bay via what is now Tennyson Road, where the Totland Bay Hotel would provide high-class accommodation for both rail and paddle-steamer travellers. However, this didn't come to be and Freshwater Station remained 'the end of the line'. Ambitious projects for a rail tunnel under the Solent to Lymington were suggested in 1901 and again in 1913, but also came to nothing.

By 1904 a direct line to 'the British Madeira' (aka Ventnor) was advertised as the Tourist Express, while popular Monday excursions ran from Freshwater to Ryde, Sandown, Cowes and

Artist's impression of Freshwater Station

Awaiting arrival of VIP at Freshwater Station

Ventnor Town, also to Wroxall, Ventnor (East), Shanklin, Brading, St Helens and Bembridge. Tickets were issued from Freshwater and Yarmouth stations for cheap day-return Pleasure Trips to various venues, with cheap half-day returns on Thursday afternoons and a 'Round the Island' tour for five shillings. A Drewry rail car, advertised for use by parties, is described as 'a little more spacious than the regular rail carriage'… terms on application.

For those travelling to London, tickets for travel from the Island on a Friday, Saturday or Sunday were valid for return on the following Monday or Tuesday, while a through parcel service was available between any Island and mainland station and Pickfords offered cartage services to any destination in the country.

The railway provided a good deal of local employment. In addition to line and station staff, two goods sidings allowed wagons for carriers such as Blake, Honnor & Jeffrey, Thomas Seed and Billy Brewer to be unloaded, and the station housed a cattle dock, water column, engine shed and two carriage sheds, although the sheds were demolished in 1927. A signal

'On Monday August 11th 1889 HRH the Princess of Wales and her two daughters arrived by special train at Freshwater. They walked to Freshwater Bay Hotel for lunch before driving to Totland where the Royal Yacht lay in the Bay...'

1889 Parish Church magazine

box brought from Newport went on to act as a bus shelter after the railway's closure, before resuming its intended role when relocated to the IW Steam Railway line at Wootton in 1987. The station house was occupied for a short time after the station closed, when a past tenant tells of gas lamps, an old black cooking range and a copper in the yard.

On the forecourt of the station Messrs Russell, Reason, and Cooper would wait at a cabby rank with horses and carriages to convey passengers to their various destinations, while WH Smith trading from station premises stored bicycles in a large shed, for use by paper boys to deliver newspapers from the early morning train. Bumble Groves would be at the station at six in the morning to collect mail for both Freshwater and Totland post offices, picking up their outgoing mail at quarter to seven in the evening for the eight o'clock train.

The 1901 census shows residents of Causeway Crossing Cottage as:

John Frude age 37 Railway platelayer.

Alice Frude age 32 Railway gatekeeper.

Alice Frude age 11.

Kate Frude age 10.

and in 1911:

John Frude age 48 Platelayer.

Alice Frude age 42.

Mabel Frude age 8.

Waiting for the carnival at the old Freshwater Station in the mid 1950s

On Thursday 12th October 1905 excited school children were granted a half-day holiday to allow them to witness the arrival of Princess Beatrice at Freshwater Station; an occasion not to be missed, to see a real princess in her finery alighting from the train at their local railway station. In later years children travelled to and from schools in Freshwater and Newport by train.

A report in the *IW County Press* dated 24th March 1888 tells how an old cottage, previously a mill, on Afton Causeway was burnt down during a gale, the fire thought to have been started by a spark from a railway engine. Occupied by Mr J.B. Tucker, the cottage had been inspected on the morning of the fire by owner George Fletcher Jones with a view to conversion to a gatekeeper's cottage, but as a poor widow had been allowed to live there rent-free for some years before and hoped to remain for some years more, Mr Fletcher Jones being 'averse to parting with such an ancient building and to turning out its tenant' had decided to build a gatekeeper's house on the opposite side of the road. However, with the original site now becoming available, a small cottage was duly built with a front door opening onto the road. A wooden footbridge erected for safe crossing over the rail tracks remained in place for only a short time.

Train approaching the Causeway from Yarmouth

In 1913 the Freshwater, Yarmouth and Newport Railway (FYN) became independent from the IW Central Railway, taking over responsibility for the 12-mile track with the support of Sir Sam Fay and Mr F. Aman. With rolling stock brought down from the Midlands, a new line with livery of polished teak started in June but sadly, despite connections with the steamer service between Lymington and Yarmouth and a well-used parcel service, wasn't a financial success. Ten years later, in 1923, the FYN line was taken over by Southern Railway. By this time Dodson's buses were running on the Island, taken over in 1921 and renamed the Vectis Bus Company. They in turn were bought by Southern Railway in 1929 and again renamed, as the Southern Vectis Omnibus Company. With cheaper fares and bus stops close to homes, the railway suffered, leading in 1953 to the FYN line, one of the last opened on the Island, being the first to close.

On the evening of Sunday 20th September 1953 engine 29, 'Alverstone', drew in to Freshwater's platform to be greeted by a huge crowd. As a bugle sounded, a squad of 'Redcoats' with muskets and a flag draped in black crepe were led by an 'officer' to the engine where a military-type

No. 24 'Calbourne' at Freshwater Station

funeral was enacted, then troops and passengers boarded the train to the sound of bugles, bells and horns. The 9.34 pm left Freshwater Station, steaming through the Causeway minutes later where a large crowd cheered and waved lamps before the crossing gates were closed for the final time.

Acorn Spring Works was built on the site of the station, to be replaced later by a supermarket. Remains of the platform and fence are visible from the car park of the Co-op and from the yard of the Garden Centre, where a brick-built station building has been taken into use. The gatekeeper's cottage remains but has been considerably enlarged.

Freshwater, Calbourne, Carisbrooke and Newport Stations no longer remain, but Ningwood and Watchingwell Station houses have been converted into private homes with Yarmouth Station buildings now a café/restaurant. The track now provides a beautiful riverside cycle way through Beckett's Copse, where Red Squirrels can be seen scampering through Hazel trees and lush foliage.

Postcard of the Causeway with All Saints' Church in the background, circa 1918

The Causeway

The Causeway crosses the River Yar some 200m from All Saints' Church on the western bank, to Afton on the east. Maps from the late 16th (Mercator 1595) and early 17th centuries (Speed 1611) show a pathway leading to a corn water mill, in existence from at least the mid 14th century and recorded at Afton in 1694, while the Ordnance Survey map of 1793 shows a water mill where water dammed in a mill pond would have been taken up by a wheel with the rise of the tide, then released back into the pond. An old water mill is recorded as being burned down in 1888, with the mill pond drained to merge with the remainder of the marsh.

The Yar was a busy working river, and dredged annually prior to the arrival of the railway and more serviceable roads. Until the mid 19th century, the only other crossing points were at Freshwater Gate and at Black Bridge.

'Coal barges would come up the river to the Causeway with the tide, and dredging took place every year.' Hilda Emmerton

A late resident wrote that at one time barges followed the Yar to unload very nearly at Freshwater Bay.

This same resident also recounted that a footbridge built with the railway was replaced by a kissing gate in 1916, and that the marsh, used by Mr John Tucker of Afton Farm to fatten Devon bullocks, was allowed to grow wild when George Fletcher Jones started development of the Afton estate. It is also said that Suffolk Punch horses were turned onto the marshy land as it was thought to be good for their hooves and that a small wharf-like area on the west bank near Freshwater Farm (now called Kings Manor Farm) was sometimes used by coal barges.

The crossing keeper's cottage, and the footbridge over tracks at the Causeway, circa 1900

Messing about on the River Yar!

In the 1940s a Sea Scout troop met at the Causeway boathouse where they had use of an ex-admiralty whaler, by courtesy of Miss May O'Conor (1896–1968). One of these ex-Sea Scouts tells how when Colonel 'Golly' Mitchell offered the troop a sail on his yacht prior to 'laying up' the lads made off enthusiastically for Lymington despite stormy weather and with the yacht rolling alarmingly before the anchor was dropped in the Lymington river.

When preparing for the return journey and the anchor was found to have become wedged, a volunteer was required to dive down and free it. This accomplished by Dave Slingsby, the sail was set for home and the calmer water of the Causeway, albeit via Newtown due to the state of the tide and strong winds. Our informant, 'volunteered' to brave the elements when it was realised the anchor hadn't been made secure, describes gingerly making his way across the deck while desperately hanging on to the hand rail as an experience he's never forgotten.

Old Thatched Cottage at the Causeway, & all Saints Church in the distance. 1885.

The old cottage at the Causeway, formerly a water mill, which burnt down in March 1888

Mr Foss's ancient dinghy, held together by several coats of lead-based paint, was also moored at the jetty and served his grandson and friends variously as a galleon with an old sheet as a sail, a speedboat when there was a good wind, a military landing craft when stuck on the mud, or a fishing boat when strawberry netting stretched across the Yar at high tide trapped small bass and mullet as the tide dropped; these were sold as bait for a few pence to fishermen at Freshwater Bay, which was quite permissible in those days.

The Causeway, now within a Site of Special Scientific Interest, attracts artists, scholars and leisure walkers who regularly enjoy treading the old rail track to Yarmouth.

'Suffolk Punch horses bred at Chessell Stud were brought down to the Crundles, especially in summer, as the marshy land was good for their hooves.' Luke Aisher

Freshwater Bay Rocks

The Stag and Arch Rocks were formed many years before any recorded history of the Bay. The first known written reference to the Stag Rock was in the early 17th century and one of the first known depictions of the Stag and Arch Rocks was an etching by George Brannon in the early 19th century.

The Stag Rock was so named from a local legend that must have begun during the time when there were large herds of deer on the Island. The story goes that huntsmen and hounds were chasing a Stag across the Downs towards the cliffs. The Stag leapt across the chasm between the cliff and the chalk stack to escape capture. The hounds tried to follow but fell to their deaths and the Stag unable to get off the Rock also perished.

The Arch Rock was formed from a cave entrance in the headland, the softer chalk surround being eroded much faster by the action of sea, wind and rain. It remained intact until the morning of Sunday 25th October 1992 when the fragile eastern support gave way during a storm, quickly followed by the arch top and western support, leaving just two stumps to show where the iconic form had once stood.

Brannon's engraving of the Arch and Stag Rocks at Freshwater Bay, 1820

Postcard of Mermaid, Arch and Stag Rocks by W.L.C Baker, circa 1970

The Mermaid Rock was formed on 23rd February 1969. An archway beneath a chalk headland, between two small coves to the east of the Arch and Stag Rocks, collapsed without warning. Luckily, this event happened during the night and not the day, when walkers might have been rambling along the popular cliff-top path. Various names were suggested for this new chalk stack in the Bay, from 'Cave Guard' to 'Butter', the latter from the small cove called Butter Bay where legend has it butter was landed by smugglers. Eventually the name Mermaid was settled on, not only because of the mythical sea creature but also from an Inn, 'The Mermaid', that was once situated on the western shore of the Bay.

'Looking out of the window that morning my son said: "Mum, the Arch Rock's just fallen down"...' Anon

An image of the three rocks, black relief on a white background, was used as an identification graphic on 'Welcome to Freshwater Bay' road signs.

The Caves Freshwater Bay. I. W.

Exploring the caves and rocks of Freshwater Bay

The remaining Rocks stand on a ledge of chalk that stretches across the mouth of the Bay. This bar has proved hazardous to shipping during stormy weather and the prevailing south westerlies. Many ships have foundered on this coastline especially in the era when craft were powered by sail.

A Norwegian Brig *Perlen* was driven ashore in October 1851, thrown against the Stag Rock and totally wrecked. A sand painting of this event can be seen in the Carisbrooke Castle Museum.

In November 1916 a large fully rigged ship *Carl* was driven by gale force winds and a high tide over the chalk ledge or bar across the Bay. It fetched up on the shingle bank in front of what was the beach house 'Glenbrook'. The crew and ship survived the beaching but due to the deep draught of the vessel and the shallowness of the chalk ledge the *Carl* was trapped. A channel had to be dynamited through the chalk bar to provide a safe passage out.

The outcrop of rocks has provided a useful perching place for many bird species safe from predatory land mammals. Great Black-backed and Herring Gulls both use the turf-topped stacks as precarious nesting sites in the spring and summer. Cormorants can be seen drying their plumage after diving in the Bay for fish. The image of them with their white feather 'collars' and spread black winged stance has earned them the local name of Isle of Wight Parson.

Due to the exposure to wind and sea spray and the build-up of nutrient-rich bird droppings on the stacks, there is very little in the way of plant life, except grass and plantain. However, two interesting species have survived. The Rock Sea Spurrey, which has dark pink flowers, and the Rock Samphire, which has yellow flowers, both bloom during the summer months.

The ledge surrounding the Rocks is uncovered at low tide and is ideal for studying the wide range of littoral marine life – from brown, red and green seaweeds to rock-dwelling barnacles, limpets and anemones. There is also an abundance of winkles that used to be harvested and sold by local fishermen. The rock pools or 'lucks' were once featured in a television programme when a teenage Simon King, who went on to become a well-known photographer and television presenter, came for a brief visit to study the marine life of the area.

The chalk ledge also provides, at low tide, a way to the cave beneath the headland and the cove beyond and of course an opportunity for a closer inspection of the Stag and Mermaid Rocks. But be aware of the incoming tide!

Great Black-backed Gulls nesting on the Stag Rock in 2010 (photo by Anna Mustchin)

Afton Down and Military Road

On Afton Down close to the old road (now a track over the golf course) that runs eastward towards Chessell and in sight of Freshwater Bay, a small group of grassy hillocks is probably all that survives of the Signal Station originally erected in the 1790s. The engraving given by Richard Livesay to Major Don of the Grand Review at Freshwater Bay on 17th June 1798 shows troops spread across the Afton Down and encompassing the area of the signal post.

The Isle of Wight was strategically important in the defence of Britain, as any invading force gaining a foothold on the Island would have easy access to attack the south coast mainland. As far back as 1638 a watch was kept by day and night on 'Freshwater Down', although this could have been at Headon Hill near Alum Bay rather than Afton Down at Freshwater Bay.

During and after the Napoleonic Wars a military presence remained deployed extensively over the Island, with trained signallers travelling from Portsmouth to Ryde by barge along with their mounts. Due to the rough crossings two signallers and two horses were necessary in case one was lost in the crossing, as frequently happened, with both signaller and horse drowned. Trying to keep both signaller and message dry was almost impossible.

Relaxing at Freshwater Bay in the 1920s

A view of Afton Down from Tennyson Down, 1904

From 1794/1795 the Government set up a line of Signal Stations along the south coast of Britain to monitor shipping movements, identify enemy vessels and communicate with defence forces by day and by night. Each station consisted of a small prefabricated hut of two rooms with a high mast to fly flags and display signal balls. In 1812, this method of signalling was reviewed, it changed to the French Method of a high pole with hinged signal arms.

Later, in June 1812, an instruction was issued stating that persons employed in signalling must be accommodated in a building on which the semaphore mast must be erected; this was not introduced immediately, only later after peace was made with France.

Brannon's engraving of the Albion at Freshwater Bay

While improvements in military and naval technology fuelled unrest with France the launch of Gloire, a French, ironclad warship, was seen as an impending threat to Britain's coastline, and the French fleet enlarging further in 1861 with 15 more ironclad ships made invasion seem even more likely.

To MAJOR GENERAL DON Commander in Chief
This Plate of the GRAND REVIEW *near*
Is inscribed, with respectfull acknowlegments.

The Grand Review, showing musket fire in the distance, 1798

Engraved by J. Walker

of the Forces in the Isle of Wight;

FRESHWATER BAY on the 17.th of June 1798.)

by his obliged humble Servant,
Richard Livesay

Lord Palmerston became Prime Minister in 1855 and determined that Britain should be better defended. He proceeded to fortify Spithead, the Solent and the Isle of Wight. Fort Redoubt at Freshwater Bay and Golden Hill Fort at Norton Green were both built between 1860 and 1870 increasing the importance of the transfer of military information between the Island, Portsmouth and London.

In 1860 when Sir Charles Seely, the first baronet, extended his property from Brook to Atherfield, he was required by Parliament to construct a road for rapid access to the southernmost coast from the western fortifications, and for defence of the chines and beaches along the south-west of the Island. The Military Road followed the course of an existing track, from Chale in the east to Freshwater Bay in the west. Sections of this track have now been lost to coastal erosion but the viaduct at Grange Chine at Brighstone survives still.

1837 Tithe map of Freshwater Bay area, showing allotment No. 948a (centre) of Signal House and garden

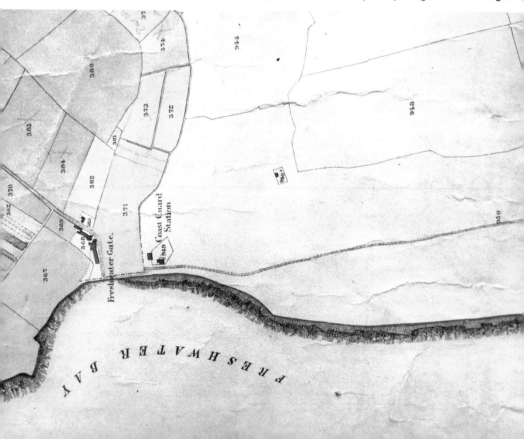

The Listening Hut on Afton Down, erected in 1917, used for early submarine detection by hydrophone

Remaining a private gated road for about 70 years, in 1930 the landowner donated the road to the Council's Highways Authority, when due to the track being vulnerable to erosion a new road was routed further inland. Re-surfaced with the labour of unemployed men turned stonebreakers, this was formally opened in March 1936. Despite the intention of maintaining the coastal Signal Stations to curtail the activity of smugglers, it seems that most were disposed of over a period of time.

The Signal Station was probably later moved from its original site on Afton Down over to the new Fort Redoubt at sometime during the late 1800s, with a new Signal Station erected on West High Down near the Needles. The site of the old Signal Station is now occupied by the underground bunker built by the Royal Observer Corps during the early 1950s at the time of the 'Cold War'.

In 1916 Admiral Jellicoe became the First Sea Lord and was determined to combat the threat of the German U-boat menace that was affecting shipping around Britain. Commander C.P. Ryan put forward a concept that he had been working on since January 1915 to track shipping movements with an electronic surveillance device, the hydrophone.

A view of Freshwater Bay, circa 1860

Following research and trials at HM Experimental Station Hawkcraig in the Firth of Forth near Aberdour, a series of 'listening huts' were established around the British coast, with one placed very close to the cliff edge on Afton Down where cables ran several miles out to sea to connect to a hydrophone in the English Channel.

The 'listening hut' housed two naval personnel, with very meagre furnishing allowing one to sleep whilst the other listened intently on headphones for any signals picked up by the hydrophone.

After the war the 'listening hut' was enlarged to become a small dwelling, but there appears to be no record of its occupancy.

Its fate was finally sealed when local Parish Councillor Captain Hall, at the Parish Council Meeting in September 1933, moved that the cliff top be acquired to prevent further building on the cliff, under the provision of the Open Spaces Act 1906, so that the view out to sea could be enjoyed by all. Soon after this, when the cliff top was acquired by the Isle of Wight Rural District Council from Sir John Seely, the hut was demolished, the site turfed and a seat placed on the cliff top for visitors and locals alike.

The site of the hut can still be seen as the banked area with the concrete manhole cover, close to the cliff edge near the Mermaid Rock.

Charles, George and William Conway

Smuggling, the Conway Brothers and Colwell Bay

The most prolific period of smuggling on the Isle of Wight took place during the 18th and 19th centuries, when there were high duties on imported goods. In the 1820s and early 1830s it took place without much hindrance. Spirits, tobacco, silk goods, lace items and tea were brought across the Channel with, at first, little danger of capture as The Revenue Service boats were no match for the smugglers.

In 1832 The Poor Law Commissioner reported the population 'was nearly all more or less concerned with smuggling'. In fact it was stated by The Coastguard Commander in 1836 that 8 out of 10 of the whole population are consumers of contraband spirits, tobacco and tea, and they consider 'there is no harm in it'.

'Smuggling was so general for a time that from all accounts there were very few homes that did not accept the offer of spirits at a greatly reduced price.' Hilda Emmerton

In the West Wight, there were a number of families that were well known for smuggling. One such family, during the mid to late 1800s, were the Conways, namely Charles (1823–1903), George (1828–1916) and William (1831–1905). They were longshoremen at Colwell Bay and many tales have been handed down about the family's exploits. According to William's granddaughter, Gertrude Turner (1902–1982), they had an intense love of the sea and adventure was in their blood. They knew every inch of the Solent, its currents, rocks and inlets. This knowledge helped enormously whilst operating their aptly named cargo vessel, *The Brothers*, in which they traded both legally and illegally!

Various members of the Conway family lived in Middleton Cottage from at least 1841 until approximately 1911 and this became one of the headquarters for their smuggling trade. Tapping sounds on the window were often heard at night by George's daughter Florence (1868–1959). She did not realise the significance of them at the time, although she had

Conway's tea cabin, with founder Jane Conway far right, 1921

Conway's flourishing business at Colwell Bay in the 1950s

heard her grandfather and great uncle going out on some unknown errand. Another house lived in by the family was Chine View, Colwell (now Chine Cottage). Being close to Colwell Bay it was an ideal location for the storage of their loot and as the Chine was much deeper then, it was quite easy to hide the tubs. In addition there were corn fields around the property where kegs could be secreted.

Extracts from Customs Prosecutions 1751–1829, held at the National Archives CUST 61/176

7 December 1822 James Ball, of Freshwater, Isle of Wight. Offence:- For carrying one cask containing 3 ½ Galls of foreign Brandy. Penalty £100. Result:- Convicted & in default of payment committed to Winchester Gaol.

3 June 1837 Henry Lane of School Green, Freshwater age 12 Offence:- Harbouring and concealing contraband goods. Result:- Fined £100 mitigated to £50 and for non-payment committed to the Common Gaol at Winchester until the Penalty shall be paid.

'Granddad couldn't swim, but he skulled a boat from Colwell Bay to Scratchell's Bay to pick up brandy smuggled from France.' Bob Acheson

Smugglers were really good at hiding the contraband goods. Sheds, hedges, gardens, wash houses, kitchens, and even churchyards were used to hide items. Table top tombs were particularly well designed for concealing goods! Many tubs were also sunk offshore, attached to long lines so they could be reclaimed at a later date, on the pretence of pulling up lobster pots. Even the gun room in the belfry at All Saints' Parish Church, Freshwater was used on occasion.

A story, as recorded in the scrapbook of the Totland Bay Women's Institute, concerns a carrier called Chambers living in Camp Road, Freshwater who used to transport the tubs to Newport. It stated that two kegs, awaiting transport, were hidden in two sacks containing potatoes, cabbages and other vegetables. Someone warned the family that the Excise men were about to call with a warrant to search the property. The sacks were quickly hidden underneath Mrs Chamber's crinoline dress whilst she stood busily washing, and a fruitless search was made of the house and outbuildings. There was a close family connection between the Chambers and Conways.

The Conway family at their home, Middleton Cottage, late 1880s

'Grandfather worked with the Totland lifeboat, but was sometimes known to row across to France bringing back illicit brandy...' Dick White

On the return to Colwell Bay, after one run, it is said that the Conway brothers misjudged the tides and they missed the intended northern shores of the Bay. Unfortunately they had to carry the tubs across an expanse of sand where they were more likely to be seen by the Coastguard 'watchers'. When all the tubs had been stacked in their 'hide', they borrowed a flock of sheep from a nearby farmer and drove them onto the sand, shepherding them up and down several times to cover their footprints. Another trick, recounted by Jack Conway (William's grandson 1904–1988), was to put the horses' shoes on the wrong way round, so misleading the Coastguards as to where the contraband goods were hidden.

One of the most popular items to be smuggled from France was brandy. The brothers used a compass set in a wooden box to navigate their passage in their open boat. They would meet up with the French farmers and buy the brandy in kegs which were then transported back. These kegs were often tied together with ropes, two at a time, suspended front and back and then brought up the cliffs over High Down (now called Tennyson Down). It was treacherous work and not without mishap. On one occasion a tub was dropped and smashed, the smell of the neat brandy wafted away on the wind! They were lucky that the Coastguards did not detect it. Florence remembered seeing her grandmother diluting and colouring some 'liquid' or 'stuff', as it was referred to, with brown sugar, having arrived uncoloured from France and having a very high alcohol content. She also remembered Aunt Sarah (1835–1927) burning ropes after being used to carry tubs up the cliff face but did not connect this with smuggling.

There were many dangers and threats for the smugglers. Whilst crossing the Channel there was the hidden threat of the sea itself and smugglers' tales tended to gloss over the anxiety of capture. If caught, and their boats were large, they were likely to be confiscated and used by the Coastguards. If small, then the boats might be cut in half (or more pieces), or some of the planks were removed from the hull, thus

COLWELL BAY, I.W.

Bathing machines at Colwell Bay, with sink and mangle bottom right, 1920s

rendering them useless. They were punished dependent on their financial and social status and the seriousness of the crime. If convicted, a fine of £100 was levied and they might be imprisoned for one year.

For the persistent smuggler the punishment was transportation or five years in the navy. In the meantime the rest of the family were left to survive somehow, perhaps even going to the 'workhouse'. By 1836 the high days of smuggling were drawing to an end. It did not finish completely but ceased to involve large numbers of the population. The Preventive men had doubled the guard between Bembridge and the Needles resulting in nine additional stations, so it was more dangerous to make the clandestine trips.

The Conways were not only longshoremen and smugglers but were involved with many aspects of local life. They volunteered for the lifeboat service when safety at sea became an important issue. In December 1859 the first formal moves were made to have lifeboat stations here and from 1860 several opened around the Island. The one at Totland Bay came into service in 1879 to keep watch over the Needles Channel and The Shingles. Several of the Conway family were amongst the volunteer crew including William's sons, Charles (1871–1957) (coxswain from 1919–1924) and Ernest (1883–1963). Sometimes the local men that made up the crew were a mix of Coastguards and smugglers, putting aside their differences when lives were at stake. The brothers played a part in the construction of the second Needles lighthouse by bringing stone from Portland in their sailing boat. Ernest was also involved in the salvage operation of HMS *Gladiator* that sank off Fort Victoria on 25th April 1908.

The Conway family were prominent at Colwell Bay for many years until 1976. The boat hire business was started by William's wife, Jane (1855–1929), during the late 1890s, probably because he was at sea a great deal and to take advantage of the increasing popularity of Colwell as a holiday location. William's sons, Charles and Ernest, continued running the business and by 1905 owned bathing machines and boats for hire. The business thrived and soon included the hire of deck chairs, beach huts and even towels! By the 1920s visitors could use a sink to rinse out their bathing costumes, a mangle to extract the water and even a line to hang the items to dry. The brothers used to fish for crabs, lobsters and prawns and then cook them over a primus stove. These were then sold to visitors or local hotels. Charles' son Jack (1904–1988) took over the business from his Dad and Uncle Ern. It was eventually sold in the early 1960s.

An information board stood near their boathouse showing whether the tide was coming in or going out. There was also a clock face with 'hands' giving the time of high tide. The Conways were very experienced longshoremen and could give advice about anything to do with the currents or local features and would keep an eye on what was happening in the Bay. They were very distinctive in their typical 'uniform' of white/navy jumper, long sea boots and a peaked cap. Sat on the bench with their backs against the Conway's boathouse and often smoking a pipe, they were popular subjects for a photograph. They were responsible for the upkeep of the beach as they owned the rights for the sand between high and low tide. Early each morning the family were seen raking over the sand and collecting up all the seaweed so the beach was tidy for the day. Ernest was a real character and left the Island on only a few occasions. He once had to attend the Coroner's Court in Winchester when someone drowned at Colwell in one of their sailing boats. During the questioning he was asked, 'Did the person know where to go?' Ernest replied, 'Well, I told him to go "up along" but he went "down along".' In other words, he was at the mercy of the tide and wind.

Jane also started a business selling teas during the late 1890s. Originally, these were served in the garden of their home at 'Chine View' under the apple tree. Jane later purchased a piece of land at Colwell Bay and an old railway carriage was erected. Conways Tea Cabin was born! By the 1920s the business also involved a putting green, where 'Longbeach' flats are now situated. The tea rooms were rebuilt by Edwin Chambers in 1932 at a cost of around £100. The wooden structure stayed virtually the same over the years apart from a few minor additions. In the beginning there was no running water or electricity and so they were only able to sell a limited range of foods and beverages.

Over the years the tea rooms have been run by several generations of the Conway family. Ernest's wife, (Lily) Rose (1894–1981), worked with her mother-in-law and then later their daughter-in-law, Margaret. The current William Conway (Bill) also served in the shop until Margaret and he both retired and the business sold in 1976 when it became known as the 'Captain's Cabin'. It continued as a tea room/café/restaurant and fancy goods shop. However, in January 2014, the building was demolished to make way for new, larger premises. Although, as Bill Conway says, 'This ends the Conway's link with Colwell Bay', the name Conway will 'live on', as it can be seen on the road sign, CONWAY LANE, off Fort Warden Road.

The Forts

After the Spanish Armada in 1588 the western Solent's defences were Yarmouth Castle on the Island, and Hurst Castle at the end of Hurst Spit on the mainland.

Between 1795 and 1805 during the Napoleonic Wars, five earth batteries were constructed on the Freshwater Peninsula and its environs, at Sconce Point, Cliff End, Compton Chine, Grange Chine in Brighstone and a barracks at Colwell Bay. These were all disarmed and abandoned after the Battle of Waterloo in 1815.

A revolution in February 1848 thrust Louis-Philippe from the French throne. He fled to England to escape the French revolution, and a republic was proclaimed in France. To further confound British observers, Louis-Napoleon was elected president in the December of the same year and in 1852 was declared Emperor, sparking another invasion panic. Lord Palmerston, when he became Prime Minister in 1855, believed that Britain needed to strengthen its defences as the south coast was vulnerable to invasion from the English Channel, particularly if the Isle of

Bathhouse side of Freshwater Bay, with Fort Redoubt on the cliff, 1920s

The gated Military Road, Freshwater Bay, early 1900s

Wight was taken. Palmerston and the Duke of Wellington being of the same mind counselled Parliament to this effect.

The then recent technological developments in the use of artillery, and the new steam-driven ironclad ships of the French Fleet, provided very effective firepower, and turned crossing the Channel into a completely different form of warfare from the Napoleonic Wars earlier in the century.

Palmerston felt that the existing defences would not withstand the onslaught of such an invasion and advised Parliament that extensive defensive improvements were required to resist this threat. As a result a total of 19 fortifications were constructed on the Isle of Wight plus a further three forts in Spithead to defend Portsmouth, all between 1850 and 1860.

'In about 1942 we went to play on the lower end of Golden Hill adjoining Heathfield Road where soldiers were using the area as an assault course. The sergeant bellowed "You boys, clear off!" but we stood our ground saying that we had played there before he ever came...' Bob Acheson

Fort Victoria from the jetty, showing the gunnery targets on the shore, circa 1910

Inland defence consisted of what was known as the Yar Stop Line, reviving an idea put forward by Sir John Oglander in the 17th century to make Freshwater Isle a place of sanctuary in the event of an invasion by allowing the sea to flood the river and so isolate the land.

The Yar Stop Line was a defensive line of fortification using the natural water obstacle of the River Yar, with pill boxes on the Peninsula side of the river where there was a road crossing, and at Freshwater Bay just behind the west end of the promenade to protect the continuance of the Military Road towards Gate Lane. Pill boxes were sited to defend the access roads across the river at Blackbridge Road, Afton Road and the Causeway, being built on solid ground just to the west of the Marshland.

The Freshwater Bay pill box was demolished after the Second World War, but three remain and can be easily spotted just alongside the 'River Walk' at Blackbridge, in the car park at 'The End of the Line' cafe in Afton Road and alongside the bridge at the Causeway.

Artillery gun at Golden Hill Fort, early 1900s

The fortifications built on the Freshwater Peninsula consisted of the following (with dates built):

Fort Redoubt at Freshwater Bay 1855–56

The Needles Old Battery at West High Down 1861–63

The Needles New Battery at West High Down 1893–95

Hatherwood Point Battery at Headon Hill 1865–69

Warden Point Battery at Colwell 1862–63

Fort Albert at Cliff End Battery 1859–77

Fort Victoria at Sconce Point 1852–55

Golden Hill Fort at Norton Green 1863–68

Tennyson Down

A walk along Tennyson Down gives one of the best views on the Island. On a clear day one can see as far as St Catherine's Point to the east, Swanage to the west, and Yarmouth and Lymington to the north.

Tennyson Down is part of the chalk ridge which runs through the centre of the Island. According to *The Penny Magazine* in 1836, the cliffs rise 'above the level of the sea, perpendicularly in some places, and overhanging in an alarming manner in others. They are for the most part perfectly white, with narrow streaks of black flint...'

E.M. Forster wrote of the cliffs from the mainland in *Howard's End*: 'So tremendous is the City's trail! But the cliffs of Freshwater it shall never touch, and the island will guard the Island's purity till the end of time. Seen from the west the Wight is beautiful beyond all laws of beauty. It is as if a fragment of England floated forward to greet the foreigner – chalk of our chalk, turf of our turf.'

East High Down, later Tennyson Down, pre 1900

East High Down, later Tennyson Down, showing Tennyson's Monument at highest point

The 1947 Ward Lock & Co guide book of the Isle of Wight states that: 'In the opinion of many this is, in good weather, the finest of all the fine walks in the Island.'

Today the downs are used for leisure, but in Victorian times both seabirds and their eggs were harvested. This was a dangerous occupation, using perilous paths or descending by means of a rope tied to a stake or iron bar driven into the top of the cliff. Worsley, in his *History of the Isle of Wight* (1781), described how a dozen birds generally yielded one pound weight of soft feathers for which the merchants (e.g. upholsterers) gave eightpence, while the carcases were bought by fishermen for sixpence per dozen, 'for the purpose of baiting their crab-pots.' Rock Samphire, growing in green tufts on the cliff face, was gathered by similar means and made into pickle by the poor.

'During war years Tennyson Down was used for training, and littered with ammunition.' Dave Kissick

Harvesting seabirds and eggs at West High Down, early 19th century (courtesy IW Records Office)

Drawn & Engr.d by Geo.Brannon.

Pub.d by Geo.Brannon. Wotton. I.W. June 2. 1823.

FRESHWATER CLIFFS, I.W.

Sketched near the WEDGE ROCK, which is a large Piece of Chalk, fixed in a most extraordinary manner between the main Cliff and an immense detached mass, of a pyramidical form.

The view of Freshwater cliffs, early 19th century (image courtesy IW Records Office)

The downs between Freshwater Bay and the Needles were once called East High Down and West High Down. Alfred Lord Tennyson (1809–1892), the poet laureate, who from 1853 lived in Farringford House at the base of East High Down, said that the air was worth sixpence a pint on the downs and walked there nearly every day, wearing his black cloak and broad-brimmed hat. Not however enjoying those who came to catch a glimpse of him, he tried to maintain some privacy by lowering the farm lane coach route to Alum Bay along the south-eastern edge of the garden and building a bridge across it that led to a summerhouse, where some of his poetry was written, and to the downs.

Old Beacon, which was replaced by Tennyson's Monument in 1897

51

Tennyson's summerhouse at Maiden's Croft, Farringford, where he wrote *Enoch Arden*

By 1869, however, the intrusion from inquisitive tourists had become intolerable and he bought Aldworth in Sussex where he spent the summers, only returning to Farringford for the winter months.

Nodes Beacon, on the highest point of East High Down (147 metres/482 feet), was a sea mark for sailors. In 1897, the old beacon was replaced by Tennyson's Monument – a Celtic cross made of Cornish granite and nearly 38 feet high. On the east face is inscribed: 'In memory of Alfred Lord Tennyson this cross is raised, a beacon to sailors, by the people of Freshwater and other friends in England and America.' The remaining stump of the old beacon was moved to the lower slope of the down, alongside a half-sized replica of the original erected by the Rotary Club of West Wight to celebrate the Queen's Silver Jubilee in 1977.

In 1927, the poet's son Hallam Tennyson presented 155 acres of the down to the National Trust in memory of his father. East High Down was renamed Tennyson Down to commemorate the poet.

The chalk downs are among the richest in the country for wildlife with Cormorants, Shags, Guillemots, Peregrines, Feral Pigeons, Ravens and Jackdaws nesting on the cliffs. Puffins once nested here but declined rapidly from the 1920s and the last breeding record was in the 1970s. As a child in the 1960s, this writer would listen for the Yellowhammer's distinctive song from the gorse 'a little bit of bread and no cheese.'

Adonis Blue butterfly on Bird's-foot Trefoil (photo Ian Pratt)

In spring the largest concentration in the country of Early Gentian grows here. Nine species of orchid are found, including the Pyramidal Orchid, the Isle of Wight county flower, while Clustered Bellflower is another speciality of the chalk. There are good colonies of butterflies, including Dark Green Fritillaries, Chalkhill and Adonis Blues.

Between Farringford and Freshwater Bay stands the only thatched church on the Island, built in 1908 on land donated by Hallam Tennyson. His wife Audrey suggested it should be named St Agnes, as she had always admired this young and beautiful Saint. The stones used to build

the church are said to have been taken from the old farmhouse at Hook Hill Farm, explaining the date of 1694 engraved on a quoin stone in the vestry wall. Robert Hooke, the famous scientist and inventor, grew up in a cottage that was later incorporated into this farm.

Alfred Lord Tennyson is buried in Westminster Abbey but his wife Emily, his son Hallam and Hallam's wife Audrey, and two grandsons are buried at All Saints' Church, Freshwater.

Pyramidal Orchid, the Isle of Wight county flower (photo Colin Haygarth)

School Green and Moa Place

School Green

In September 1714, Colonel David Urry of Easton bequeathed land in the old 'tun' of Middleton for a school for 16 poor children of the Parish where they would be taught 'reading, writing and ciphering'. In April 1715, David Lacey was appointed the school's first schoolmaster. The school bore the inscription 'The Gift of Col Urry' and was called the Urry School. It stood on land now occupied by the shops at Moa Place. The area where the school was situated became known as School House Green or School Green and a hamlet of shops and houses grew up around the school.

The population of Freshwater Parish remained at 600 throughout the 18th century, but by the mid 1840s it had grown to 1,460, and 129 pupils were being taught at the Urry School. A larger school building was clearly needed. In 1848, Benjamin Cotton of Afton Manor bought part of a field called Long Half Butt as a gift for a new National School a quarter of a mile east of the old school and this opened in January 1851. Freshwater's population continued to rise rapidly during the mid to late 1800s, partly due to the building of the forts from the early 1850s, and children of troops garrisoned there attended the school. By 1906, it was known as All Saints' School and 340 children (up to age 14) and 135 infants were taught there.

The road leading from School Green alongside the brook to the east was called Doves Lane until the late 1800s, after a family called Dove who lived there. It then became Station Road when the railway came and some years after the railway had gone it was renamed School Green Road in reference to the old school and the hamlet of School Green.

Moa Place and the New Zealand connection

Moa Place, Timarue Place, Hokitika and Omarue are the names of buildings in the middle of Freshwater. Why do they have these New Zealand names?

The old schoolhouse at School Green in the late 1880s, when converted into two cottages

The man responsible for building these shops and houses was George Scorey, who was born near Lymington in 1846. In 1868, George set sail from London for Christchurch, New Zealand with other European settlers. He was in New Zealand less than eight years but made money there that enabled him to have a better life when he returned to England.

By 1876 George was back in England and running a pub in Southampton with his wife Celia. One of George's six brothers married a Freshwater girl in 1880 so perhaps George realised the potential of Freshwater for speculative building then. By 1885 he had built the Assembly Rooms at School Green as a place to provide entertainment to the growing and increasingly fashionable population. Here concerts, lectures and balls were held and plays performed. George's father, another George, moved down from Winchester to run the Assembly Rooms.

About the same time, George built Timarue Place, with two shops and living accommodation, next door to the Assembly Rooms. Florence Elliott ran a newsagents and stationers in one of these shops between 1900 and 1954, and a shop called Elliott's exists there today. George also built a row of houses next to Timarue Place. These were called Hokitika, Wanganui, Opawa and Omarue, all New Zealand place-names.

School Green Road circa 1903 showing Moa Place, built in 1896 by George Scorey

George bought the Royal Standard Hotel and installed his brother Walter as landlord in 1892. He bought the Vine Inn in 1891 and brother Frank was landlord there between 1901 and 1911. By 1896, George had knocked down the two ramshackle cottages that had once been the Urry School and replaced them with a distinctive row of four shops. These he called Moa Place after an extinct type of New Zealand bird. Moas were unable to fly and had been hunted by the Maori until they died out around 1500. They resembled an emu or ostrich and the largest of the species, the Giant Moa, stood at 3 metres high and was the tallest bird that ever lived.

Sadly, George died in Southampton in 1898 aged just 52. George senior, Walter and Frank continued to live in Freshwater with their wives and children and 18 properties in School Green continued to be owned by the Scorey family into the 1920s.

The Assembly Rooms became the Palace Theatre in 1908 and this was run by Cecil Elgar (nephew of the famous composer Sir Edward Elgar) and W.G. Barnard. This burnt down in 1929 and Kempsters drapers and outfitters shop replaced it in 1934 after the business moved from Simmons Corner, Victoria Road. This closed in 1995 and was sold to the Tudor Lounge restaurant. In 2008, it became Hong Kong Express.

Edward VII commemorative trees

To mark the coronation of Edward VII in 1902, an oak tree known as the 'Coronation Oak' was planted on the triangular green in front of Moa Place. Sadly, this does not appear to have survived for long. Much longer-lasting were the 30 or more commemorative Horse Chestnut trees planted along School Green Road, Brookside Road and Queens Road. Their white flower 'candles' produce a stunning display in May. Unfortunately, some of these trees became diseased in the first decade of the 21st century and have had to be removed. Walnut trees have been planted in their place.

The green alongside the brook is manorial land as it was presented to the village by the Tennyson family. It should not be enclosed or built on. In spring, a wonderful display of daffodils, snowdrops and crocuses can be seen on the banks of the brook. These were planted from the late 1950s. There were also rose beds on the green in the 1960s and 1970s.

Spring bulbs and Horse Chestnuts along the brook at School Green Road in March 2014 (photo by John Noyce)

Freshwater Library

The County Seely Library opened in Newport in 1904 and book collections were sent out in boxes four times a year and displayed at West Wight Social Club and in local schools. In 1936, West Wight councillor Miss May O'Conor raised concerns about this system of providing library books to local residents and the County Council subsequently agreed to the erection in Freshwater of the first purpose-built branch of the Seely Library. A piece of land known as Cooper's Field, a popular children's playground as well as a source of animal dung used by locals as fuel, was purchased from the owner, Florence Plumley, as a site for the new library. The building design was New England Colonial, mainly of timber with a pantiled roof, set back from the road and in attractive grounds. Due to the imminence of war, shutters were added at the doors and windows for 'blackout' purposes. The opening ceremony was performed on 16th November 1939.

Freshwater Library (originally West Wight Seely Library), 1950s

Robert Hooke and Hook Hill Farm

Robert Hooke, one of the most important scientists of the 17th century, was born in Freshwater in July 1635, the fourth child of John Hooke, curate of All Saints' Church. The family lived in a cottage that later became part of Hook Hill Farm. Robert's father died in 1648, and Robert was then schooled in London before going on to Oxford University. He made important discoveries in many different fields, including astronomy, biology, geology and physics, and was an inventor and architectural surveyor.

Longhalves Lane towards Hooke Hill; Longhalves Cottage is now one dwelling but was three farm labourers' cottages in 1861

The road running past Hook Hill Farm was not originally named after the Hooke family, who spelt their surname differently. It has been suggested that Hook Hill was so named because it was situated at a bend in the River Yar; but it could equally have been named after the sharp bend in the road. After Hook Hill Farm was abandoned in the late 1890s, the old stone buildings were removed and some of the stone was used to build St Agnes' Church at Freshwater Bay in 1908. A house called Heatherstone now occupies the site.

In the mid 1960s, the Freshwater Parish Council agreed that Robert Hooke should be commemorated in some way and the spelling on the road sign was changed to 'Hooke Hill'. A block of Cornish granite that had originally formed part of a mounting for a muzzle-loading cannon at Hatherwood Battery was used as a memorial stone and placed at the bottom of the hill outside Acorn Spring Works (now the Co-op supermarket). The memorial was unveiled in July 1966 by Earl Mountbatten of Burma.

Longhalves Lane

This ancient footpath runs from Hooke Hill to the Vine Inn. On the 1793 OS map, long narrow fields enclosed by hedges can be seen running from north to south between the lane and what is now School Green Road. These strips of land are roughly half an acre each – hence the name Longhalves. They are thought to be the remnants of a planned medieval village built shortly after the Norman Conquest. In a planned medieval village, each family was allocated half an acre of land in a long narrow plot, one end of which faced the street. Each plot had a dwelling and outbuildings with an area for livestock, vegetables or orchards. It is thought that this settlement would have been deserted sometime before the 16th century – perhaps as a consequence of the Black Death or after attacks by the French.

Bibliography and Sources

Aisher, Luke

All Saints' Church Magazine

British Museum

Buisseret, David. 'A Belgian Family in the Isle of Wight'

Catford, Nick. 'Disused stations: closed railway stations in the UK'.
www.disused-stations.org.uk

Conway, William Charles (Bill) and Margaret

Cowes & Isle of Wight Customs History www.customscowes.co.uk

Emmerton, Hilda

Foskett, Graham

Foss, Keir

Frazer, Oliver. 1990. *The Natural History of the Isle of Wight*. Dovecote Press, Wimborne

Freshwater Parish Archives

Freshwater, Yarmouth & Totland Advertiser

Green, Doreen

H2g2. h2g2.com/Fortifications of the Isle of Wight

Hastings Chronicle

Hurt, John. 2000. *300 Years of Education in Freshwater: a celebration of 150 years of All
Saints C.E. (controlled) Primary School 1850–2000*. West Island Group, Freshwater

Hutchings, Richard J. 1985. *Smugglers of the Isle of Wight*. Isle of Wight County Press Ltd

Martin, Rob. Robert Hooke website.
http://freespace.virgin.net/ric.martin/vectis/hookeweb/roberthooke.htm

Isle of Wight Council. 'Freshwater Library – a brief history'.
www.iwight.com/azservices/documents/1568-75Years.pdf

Isle of Wight County Archaeology and Historic Environment Service. *Historic Environment
Action Plan – Freshwater Isle*

Isle of Wight County Press

Isle of Wight County Records Office. Freshwater Valuation Book 1920

Johnstone, Joy. M. 1993. *Fall of the Arch Rock*. Seawinds Services

Jones, Jack & Johanna. 1987. *The Isle of Wight: an illustrated history*. Dovecote Press,
Wimborne

Margham, John. 1994. Freshwater – man and the landscape.
Isle of Wight Natural History and Archaeological Society 12: 95–124

Medland, John C. 1986. *Shipwrecks of the Wight*. West Island Printers

Medland, John C. 1995. *Alum Bay and the Needles*. Coach House Publications Ltd

National Trust. www.nationaltrust.org.uk

Parr, Donald A. 1996. *Britain in Old Photographs: the West Wight*. Sutton Publishing Ltd

Penny Magazine 1836

Readers Group of Companies. www.readersgroup.com/readers_history.htm

Smithers, Judith. The Conway family archive book

Steere, Stephen. Scorey one-name study. The Guild of One-Name Studies, London

Ward Lock & Co. Guide Book of the Isle of Wight for 1947

Westcott Jones, K. *The Railway Magazine*, May and June 1947

Whittingham, John

Wilson, H. W. 1920. *'Hush' or the Hydrophone Service*. Mills & Boon Ltd

For supplying photos or artwork, we thank R. Acheson, D. Buckett, I. Hales, H. Humber and R. Ninnis.